10 MINUTE
TRANSFORMATIONS

to help you declutter and
get organised

George Tanner
Simplify By George

"Organising is what you do before you do something, so that when you do it, it is not all mixed up."

— A A Milne

I would like to thank everyone who has supported me on my journey, but with special thanks to:

Mum & Dad - who have provided so much support over the years

Neil & Jake - for always believing in me & encouraging me to chase my dream

Verity - the friend everyone should have

Thank you all Gx

CONTENTS

CHAPTER 1

INTRODUCTION

The thought of trying to declutter or get organised can be overwhelming. When I was younger, I used to reorganise my room regularly (yes, the signs were there from an early age). I emptied the contents of my room onto the floor then soon got distracted by a book or some photos... and suddenly it would be time for tea; there I would be, surrounded by a pile of stuff, unable to walk across the room. Obviously this is not a good starting point, and since then I have discovered that the secret to decluttering and getting organised is to do little and often.

Since launching Simplify By George, I have been driven by the desire to make decluttering and organising accessible to everyone. Two years ago, I launched Well Organised Wednesdays, short and achievable activities to help organise your home. This book is a collection of those activities - designed to take 10 minutes or less - that will transform an area of your home, one activity at a time.

This book is structured room by room, allowing you to either move through the book chronologically or pick a room you want to start with or jump to the index to find a category depending on what is bothering you the most, or what suits your mood that day. It has the added benefit of giving you guidance on what, based on my experience, could go where. Following each activity, if you have more time and energy, I have included further ideas on how to continue your journey to getting organised; some are short activities and others that may take a little longer.

Before you dive in and get started, here are a few things to remember:

- The activities are only 10 minutes each but do make sure you give yourself that time and are free from distraction - you don't want to find your bed covered in clothes when you want to go to sleep.
- Use boxes to help you contain items and give structure, they don't have to be elaborate - shoe and mobile phone boxes are great to use.
- Label, label, label. It helps you to remember where things should go and helps everyone else in the house maintain all your hard work.
- Donate or sell anything you would be happy to buy yourself – the final chapter of this book lists some great organisations you can donate items to.

I hope you find this book useful in transforming and organising your home, you'll be amazed by how much you can achieve, 10 minutes at a time.

CHAPTER 2

ENTRANCE HALL

This is one of the most important, but challenging, places in your home in which to create order. The doorway into your home, it gives the first impression, greeting everyone who walks into your house. Despite this it inevitably ends up as the dumping ground for everything, shoes, coats, bags, and all manner of other things. This chapter looks at the following items:

Coats

Shoes

Bag

Hates, Gloves & Scarves

Keys

COATS

Your coats and jackets are probably in various places dotted around your house, by the door, under the stairs, in your wardrobe or even in your car. To start this transformation the first thing to do is gather them all together in one place. Once you've done this it is much easier to review what you have, what you need and what you really could let go of.

Have a look at the coats and see if they are:
- too small,
- too big,
- not the right colour,
- not a style you like.

Now be honest. Put them on and see how you feel when you do - are you smiling or are your shoulders slumped?

Make three piles– keep, donate, and discard.

- The discard pile are ones you don't want to wear and that are not in good enough condition to sell or donate - they can go straight into the bin.
- Donate any that are in good enough condition (see donate chapter).
- Now all you need to do is find new homes for the keep pile. If you've had enough at this stage, just pop them back where they came from. If you want to go a step further the next activity looks at where you keep your coats and how to get them organised.

Ready for more?
The main problem with the entrance hall is there are usually too many coats for the space. The only way to keep this space tidy is to review what coats you need at hand and which ones can be stored elsewhere.

Before starting this make sure you've completed the previous activity for every member of the household, so that you're only looking at how to store what you are keeping. Once you've done that you'll easily be able to pull out the coats you wear daily. These are the ones you should store by the door; the rest can be stored in individual wardrobes.

Remember, this will change with the seasons, you don't need to keep all the rain, winter, and summer jackets in one space. If space in a wardrobe becomes tight you can store your out of season coats and jackets in a vacuum bag under your bed, or in the spare room.

Once you have identified the coats and jackets you are wearing right now you can assess the space you have available to hang them.

If you have younger children think about putting hooks at a height they can reach, this can be a row of hooks under your existing ones, it will not only encourage them to hang up their coats when they come in, it also cunningly doubles the amount of space available.

If you are still struggling for space, look at what you have chosen to keep out; any more than two coats per person is going to cause issues, especially in the winter, maybe you only have room for one. Make adjustments and hang what you need, this will reduce the bulky coat clutter in the hallway.

SHOES

Shoes are another item that tend to be spread around the house. Storing them is an issue for everyone. Before you worry about where to put them, the first thing is to make sure you are only thinking about the ones you want to keep; this is your 10 minute transformation.

Find all your shoes, look through them and make three piles:
- ones you wear that are in good condition,
- ones you would wear but need repairing (heels etc)
- ones you no longer wear, find uncomfortable, are falling apart or you just no longer like.

Let's start with the ones you no longer wear; these can easily make up two piles - ones to be thrown away (pop them straight in the bin) and the rest to donate. There are lots of places you can donate shoes, check out the donate chapter at the end of this book. The important thing with these shoes is to get them out of the house as quickly as you can so they don't clutter up your hallway (or the boot of your car).

The same goes for any shoes that need repairing, get them to your local repair shop asap so you can get them back and start wearing them. Be realistic with these shoes, if you haven't been able to get them to the repair shop for months, maybe it is something you will never have time to do, in which case just get rid of them.

Now move onto the ones you are keeping, this will take slightly longer, so if your 10 minutes is up you can pop them back where you got them and come back to this later.

Ready for more?
First you need to complete the shoe activity for all your family, then you can clearly see the size of the problem. A lot of people would love to keep all their shoes together in the entrance hall, but that's usually impractical due to the sheer number of shoes a whole family owns and the space available. Here is how to organise them.

With your less frequently used shoes, store them somewhere you can easily access if you need to, for example the bottom of your wardrobe or under the bed. There are lots of good shoe storage options available that will keep them contained and dust free, you just need to measure the space and do some research.

Now you are left with your everyday shoes. Store these as close to the door as possible (this could be under the stairs), in appropriate shoe storage. To do this look at the space you have and how many pairs of shoes you want to store.

Measure the space and search for the right shoe storage; there are so many options available you will be able to find something that fits.

If you are struggling with the space not being big enough for the shoes you have then look at how many shoes you have kept out for frequent use. Any more than two pairs per person is probably too much, you may only have space for one, reassess and look again.

Now all you have to do is encourage everyone to put their shoes away when they come in. Good luck!

BAG

Loads can be stored in one bag, they are used all the time after all... but how often have you dared to empty yours out to make sure you are only carrying what you need? Now's the time to be bold and tip it all out onto a table and sort the contents into:

- what you need in the bag, be honest,
- rubbish and dirty tissues, these can go straight into the bin.

Look at what is left, do you really need a piece of Lego or small plastic toy? It might be an essential part of your tool kit when you are out, or it may have strayed in there without meaning to, assess it and decide if you need it.

Think about if there is something useful you had forgotten or lost? Has your stock of masks run out, or have you misplaced the trolley £1? Find what you need and put all the contents in your bag. Your bag is now transformed!

Ready for more?

If you want to do a bit more, think about all your bags. As with shoes and coats you will probably have more than one. The best place to keep your daily bag is in the entrance hallway (a row of hooks under your coats works well for bags, including school bags).

For all your other bags the wardrobe is the best place, but before you shove them all in, have a quick check, do you still use them all? Do you even like them? Donate any you no longer want. Those you are keeping can be stored on a shelf or in a drawer.

HATS, GLOVES & SCARVES

A seasonal item that is great to have near the door so that they are easy to find on the way out and when you come in it's quick to pop them back. First go and find them from the various hiding spots, time to look through them:

- are the gloves in pairs?
- are there any holes?
- do the hats fit?
- does everyone have at least one of everything?

Anything you don't need can be thrown away or donated (see donate chapter), then store the rest. You can use old shoe boxes if they are in a cupboard or if they are going to be on show you might want to invest in something that looks more attractive. You can either store them by type i.e., gloves in one box, hats in another or you can have a box for every person. Do what works for you and the space you have, if possible make them easily accessible for younger family members to encourage them to find and put them away by themselves.

KEYS

Everyone has spare keys somewhere (usually in the hall console or junk drawer), some of those will be for doors you no longer have. This activity is to test all those keys against the doors in your home and then to keep them together in a place that makes sense.

- First find all the keys, then sort through them:
- Keep and label the ones you need (you can label with stickers or bits of paper and tape, use abbreviations or first names if you are holding onto friends or neighbours' keys.
- Let go of the rest, you can pop them straight in the recycling.

This can feel uncomfortable to do as the risks seem high, but the chances are if you don't know what they are for you never will and you don't need them anymore.

Finally find a pot for the labelled keys you want to keep and pop them in a place that makes sense.

CHAPTER 3

SITTING ROOM

The one room we would most love to be a sanctuary - a place to escape to when the day is done, to relax, unwind and reset - is often the one that can most easily get out of control. It is home to many things, everyone in the house uses the space so there tends to be a lack of ownership in keeping it organised. This chapter covers the most common objects found in this space, some of these may also be in your kitchen if you have a large open plan social space.

Books

Games

CD's / DVD's

Magazines & Papers

BOOKS

If you own beautiful bookshelves crammed with books you love, this activity is going to be a tough one. There is no 10 minute activity that is going to transform your bookcase, but there are some things you can do to kick off the process.

Stand in front of your bookcase and spend 10 minutes finding books:

- You have started and never finished (if you are a completer finisher you may feel compelled to hang onto them, but if you haven't finished them yet, try and let them go otherwise they will be a constant reminder of something you haven't done), once you have let them go you will not give them a second thought.
- You will never re- read.
- You have had since childhood, know your children are not interested in, and don't want to hold onto for sentimental reasons.

- Are left over from your studying days; they may have been interesting at school / university, but they'll now be out of date and you won't need them again.

Books can inspire an abundance of emotions, but guilt and duty should not be among them. This is a perfect time to make room on your shelves for some new treasures and donate the ones you don't want so someone else can find and love them.

Ready for more?

If you want a true transformation of your bookshelves, the only way to do it is to clear the shelves completely and look at each book one by one. Decide whether it should stay or go (the same reasons as before). When you put them back organise them in a way that works for you; by author, subject or you could even try styling them by size or colour which makes for a stunning display.

GAMES

Board games can congregate in various places, from the kitchen to children's rooms through to sitting rooms. It sometimes makes sense not to have everything together especially when you use them in different places, but the sitting room is a good central place to store the majority as it is where a lot of games are played as a family. To start this activity, gather all your family games and sort into the following:

- The ones you know are played regularly; this is your keep pile.
- Ones that have pieces missing or are broken, put them in a pile to recycle what you can and throw what you can't (it is always good to keep a few extra counters or dice in case others go missing from games you like).

Look at what is left; if you are not sure about it have another quick look at it:

- If you have not played it because the instructions seem to be complicated are you ever going to?
- If you are still not sure put these games to one side and try to play them in the next few weeks, it will help you decide if you want to keep them or not.

It's worth being as honest and realistic as possible about this – sometimes holding on to things in the hope you will use them or play them one day is just setting yourself up to feel like a failure – it can be liberating to admit if you really are never going to play that game then get rid of it!

You can donate the ones you are not going to play and enjoy the ones you love.

CD'S / DVD'S

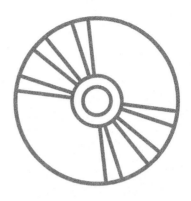

If you are a streamer, this is a quick activity – let them all go.

If you are struggling to do this it might help to shift how you think about them. These are items which have a large sunk cost value attached to them, you remember buying them for anything from £5 to £19.99, it feels like an awful lot of money, and this makes them hard to throw away. There's also the emotional memories and associations with certain music and films. But if you are not using them, they are gathering dust and taking up valuable space – not only physically but also in your brain. There are loads of places where you can sell or donate them, check out the donate chapter.

If you do watch or listen to them you can quickly identify the ones you always pick up, they will inevitably be the ones that are not in their cases. The ones you don't watch/ listen to will be tucked away safe and sound in their cases.

You can get rid of ones you no longer use (see donate chapter) and then look at the ones you are keeping and how you store them. Generally, they don't make an attractive display and take up a lot of room, if you put them in a CD wallet it reduces the space as well as allows you to tuck them away neatly in a cupboard or behind the sofa. If you don't like the idea of taking them out of their cases, find a drawer you can store them in. Store them vertically, it takes up less space as well as allowing you to easily find the one you want.

MAGAZINES & PAPERS

If you like the printed form you may have a few magazines or papers at home, and they will probably be in various places so collect them all together and go through them.

- If you haven't read it yet have to look at why not and be honest. Maybe you haven't had time and it feels wasteful to throw away the past two months of unread magazines. If this is the case and you cannot bring yourself to throw them away just now, set yourself a deadline to do so and if you haven't by then put them straight into the recycling. Unread magazines and papers can feel like another thing to do, they are something you do not need to add to your list.

- If you are keeping it for that one article or recipe - just rip it out, put it in a folder and chuck the rest.

- If you have read it and just not got around to throwing it away, now is the time – you can put them straight into the recycling, or if you have time drop them to a neighbour you know might appreciate them, or the local doctors' surgery.

The last thing to do is to find somewhere to store the ones you are going to read, so they have a place to belong, remember to contain in a box or file.

CHAPTER 4

KITCHEN

The heart of the home, this is the room where everything happens. It is so often a multi-purpose room not just designed for cooking but also eating, entertaining, playing and generally hanging out. It is the most overwhelming room to get organised but the flip side of this is it is the most satisfying once it is. Getting this room to function and work for you, not against you, can make life much easier for everyone.

Whilst there is a lot to do, it is also easy to break down into smaller activities which makes it more manageable to approach. In this chapter we will cover:

Food	Mugs	Tupperware	Alcohol
Freezer	Tea & Coffee	Utensils	Medicine
Spices	Glasses	Tea Towels	Junk Drawer
Baking	Water Bottles	Recipe Books	

FOOD

It is easy to buy something at the supermarket for a specific recipe just in case you don't have it at home which means cupboards can easily get out of control. This activity will help you get right to the back of your cupboards and find any tins or packets of food that are past their best as well as food you know you will never eat.

- Empty everything out.
- Check the dates as you go, if you find anything past its best put it to one side to go into the bin.
- Anything close to the date put in a separate pile (to go near the front of your shelf).
- Anything that you look twice at and think you won't use put to one side (it can go to a local foodbank or to school as part of the harvest festival collection).

Now group what you have into categories (soups, beans etc), wipe over the shelf and pop them back in. Remember to put the ones that need to be used first near the front.

If you really want to be organised, you can make a list of what you have as you go, keep it on your phone so it is always handy when you are out and about. Remember this only works if you keep it up to date.

FREEZER

What is inside your freezer? Do you even know, or has it become a place you just run to for the odd ice cream or to get the peas? This is another place things get put with the full intention of using them up, but often get left there too long. The best way to sort the freezer is to tackle it drawer by drawer.

- Take everything out.
- If it does not have a label and you don't know what it is, you are never going to reach for it, it is time for it to go (alternatively, if you are overwhelmed by wasting food and feel brave you could pop all the unknown items in your fridge and have a game of freezer roulette over the next few nights).
- If you don't know how old it is, or if there is evidence of freezer burn it is time to say goodbye.
- If you put leftovers in there as you were going to eat them (but never did), then be honest and say goodbye.

Moving forward there are lots of ways you can keep your freezer organised:

- Use different drawers for different food categories.
- Always make sure you label and date your food.
- Use the same brand of Tupperware so it stacks well.
- Use silicone pouches that can stand vertically or lie flat helping to maximise space. They are reusable so much better than single use plastic bags.
- Make a list of what is in there (with dates), so you make sure you use it.

You should now have a transformed freezer.

SPICES

A recent survey suggested there are £240m of unused herbs and spices in kitchens in the UK alone. Out of date spices won't make you ill, they just don't pack the same punch, so you need to use more. That said if you have something that is more than a year old it will be past its best and it suggests you don't use it, so why keep it?

Spices tend to breed and spread all around the kitchen so the first thing to do it get all your spices together.

- Check the dates and get rid of anything older than a year. If it is something you use make a note to replace it, but if not you probably bought it for that one recipe, so it can go.
- If there are any you know you don't use throw them away.
- If you have duplicates of anything see if it is possible to decant into one jar (if the dates allow it).
- If you are feeling ready to get uber organised make a note of dates that are close and challenge yourself to use it before it expires.

Ready for more?

If you want your spices really organised it is good to think about where you store them. Ideally you want to locate spices near to your hob, so they are close at hand when you cook. Find a space where they will all fit and move what is in that space somewhere else.

A drawer is a great way to store spices, it allows you to clearly see what you have (rather than being lost at the back of a cupboard). Either lie them flat, if the drawer is shallow, or stand them up if it is deeper. You can pop a sticker on any that do not have a label on top.

If you want to totally transform the space, you can decant into jars so they all look the same, alternatively buy the same brand, this can have a similar effect without additional spend.

BAKING

Love it or hate it, you will probably have turned your hand to baking at some point, whether a birthday cake, school cake sale or something else. In your kitchen you will have various baking supplies you have enthusiastically snapped up that are potentially languishing in the back of the cupboard. Your baking equipment will probably be squeezed into various cupboards and spaces. This activity will help you transform your cupboards.

- Find all your flour, sugar, icing, baking powder and anything else you have bought and check the dates.
- Throw away anything that is not in date or anything bizarre you bought to make a certain cake that you have never used again.
- Now try to find a space where you can store them all together, if you are a keen baker you may want this to be accessible, if not then do not use one of your prime spaces. Pop them in a high cupboard so they are all together and you can reach them if you need to.

Ready for more?

Find all the baking tins you use and locate them in the same space as the ingredients. It is helpful having a baking cupboard whether you are an enthusiast or not, you can easily see what you have and what you need to get. If you are storing in a cupboard that is less accessible, storing ingredients in boxes helps you access what you need easily.

MUGS

Everyone has a favourite mug; the one you always reach for. In between your favourite mugs there are probably ones you are not bothered about and ones you just don't like (you may also have enough mugs for the whole street to come in for a cup of tea). Sorting through your mugs can make room on your shelves so you don't have to stack your mugs on top of each other or fight to close the cupboard.

- Take out all the ones you and your family love and put them to one side.
- Take out all the ones you really do not like and put them in the donate pile.
- Look at what you have left and think about how many you need before you put the dishwasher on, maybe 10-20? Select the ones you most like from this pile and donate the rest.

- The final thing is to put them all back on the shelf, remember to put the ones you love near the front or on the lower shelf (if you have more than one).
- The rest can be donated.

Ready for more?

Have a look where you have located your mugs, have you put them near the kettle and tea and coffee? If you have, well done. If not, this is something that simplifies life; locate them together.

Start next to your kettle, is there is a cupboard close by where you could locate your mugs? Is there space for all the tea and coffee? If not, is there a drawer you can find close by they could go in?

This activity will take a little longer than just sorting through them as you will need to relocate what is currently in that space, but it will be worth the effort.

TEA & COFFEE

This might be an easy task for you if you only have one type of coffee and tea; for most people there is usually an eclectic mix of teas from herbal to smoked and maybe lots of different types of coffee too. So as always, the first job is to pull them all out of the cupboard, even the ones buried right at the back.

- Check the dates and throw any old ones away.
- Pick up your favourites, put them to one side.
- Look at what is left, do you drink them, or are they there for your visitors? Keep what you know will get used and lose the rest.

Unless you are going to decant into storage jars, there is no elegant way to store tea and coffee. If you have the space, putting them in a drawer makes them far easier to see and access, but if not, stacking them in a cupboard is the only way. Make sure you put your favourites at the front and the rest at the back

Ready for more?

Have a look at where you are storing them. The best place to have tea or coffee is by the mugs and the kettle / coffee machine, so if you have a little more time, have a reshuffle and move things around. You will find making a cup of tea much easier.

GLASSES

Drinking, wine, beer and even shot glasses. There are so many types all used for different occasions and possibly stored in multiple locations (which is fine if it makes sense). If you have a lot of glasses you may find it easier to tackle one category at a time.

- Take out all your glasses, remove any which are chipped, or that you don't like drinking out of.
- Look at the space available to store them, if there is not enough room to put them back in without stacking, then maybe box up a few and store them somewhere else.

Glasses are good to hold onto (if you have excess) as they are constantly being broken or chipped. The key to it is not keeping them all in your main cupboard. Give your glasses some room and store the rest ready for when they need replacing.

Ready for more?

Look at where you are storing your water glasses, are they near the tap? If not this is a great extension activity to do, relocate everything in the nearest cupboard and pop your glasses in there, drinking will never be the same again!

WATER BOTTLES

A reusable water bottle is so much better than single use plastic, but they do have a habit of multiplying. This activity helps you think about how many you need and clear some space in your cupboards.

- Collect them all together.
- Match lids and bottles.
- Count the people in your house and the water bottles - pick a reasonable number to keep (1 each with a couple to spare?).
- Pick out your favourites.
- Get rid of the rest, either donate or discard.

Find a shelf to put them on, you can either stand them up with the lids on (or in a container by the side) or invest in a water bottle organiser there are plenty available online the majority of which are stackable, so allow you to make the most of your space.

UTENSILS

Six corkscrews, two can openers, the special thing you bought to chop herbs, a broken wooden spoon, does this sound like your utensil drawer? Do you find it jams every time you try and open it, or that everything comes out when you try to get a spoon out of the container by the hob? We all have far too many utensils and let's face it you could get by on a fish slice and wooden spoon. You can easily transform this area and make it less stressful in 10 minutes.

- Empty your utensil drawer / container.
- Pick out your top ten utensils and put them to one side.
- Pick out your five least used or useless utensils and put them into another pile.
- Look at what you have left, rank them in order of how much you use them, are there any near the 'not used in ages' end that you can get rid of?

Once you have them all sorted make sure your most used utensils are the easiest to access, put them at the front of your drawer, or in your container by the hob and place the rest somewhere you can access them.

TUPPERWARE

Tupperware (a necessary evil) is useful but a problem to store. There is no magic solution but there are some things you can do to help you keep on top of it all.

- Check you have matching containers and lids; tupperware regularly separates from its component part so doing a regular check means you always know there will be a lid for the tub you have just decanted into.
- Discard anything that does not, containers without lids can come in handy to organise drawers but if you cannot see a use for it straight away then get rid of it, it will just become clutter.

Once you have completed your check you can look at storage. You might use it regularly, but it doesn't need to be in the most accessible place as you don't reach for it every day. It will, however, always need more room than you think.

If you have room the best way to store it is with the lids on, it makes it easier to reach for the one you want. If you are tight for space stack them inside each other with their lids beside them.

The best tip for keeping tupperware organised is to always buy the same brand, that way they stack well in the cupboard or fridge.

TEA TOWELS

You have too many, you know you do as you can't shut the drawer you keep them in. You also hardly ever use them as you have a dishwasher, so apart from the Sunday roast they don't get used that much.

Get them all out, pick out 5, 6, 7 or even 8 of your favourite's, then ditch the rest.

It is good to practise the art of file folding with tea towels, they take up far less room in your drawer, you might even be able to make room for something else.

Make them into a long rectangle and then fold at least three times, until it is a little parcel that will stand up on its own. If your drawer is not very deep you may need an extra fold. They will then be filed into your drawer ready for use.

RECIPE BOOKS

How many recipe books do you have versus how many you use? It is easy to have more than you use, you may have been gifted some or, full of great intentions, decided this was the year you were going veggie or going to cook more. They are so easy to hold onto as 'there is that recipe that looks amazing' and there is a real joy in flicking through them, but if they are taking up valuable space, or make you feel guilty for not using them it is time to let go of the ones you no longer need.

- Get all your books together.
- Look at them one by one.
- If there are recipes you use put it on the keep pile.
- If you have never tried any recipes from it and know you won't it is time to donate it.

If there is a recipe you have intended to do and have not - be honest are you ever going to?

- If the answer is no, donate.

- If the answer is yes, then set yourself a target to do it, if it hasn't been done by that date then let it go.

Hopefully you should end up with a pile of books to keep and some to let go, now all you need to do is put them on a shelf together somewhere; whether on show or tucked away in a cupboard it doesn't matter, just make sure they are all together.

Ready for more?

If you have a pile of magazine cut outs and recipe cards, you can get these organised. Treat yourself to a nice folder and organise them by food types or meals so they are easier to find. Make sure you are only keeping the ones you will use; you can set yourself a target to do this.

ALCOHOL

With lots of kitchens being used as the main social space most alcohol seems to have found its way into a cupboard or a shelf in here (you might also have it stored in the sitting or utility room so this activity may take you to a different room). What is guaranteed is you will have a least one weird bottle of spirits in the house you bought on holiday because 'it was sooo good' but for some reason it doesn't quite taste the same when you get back home, or lots of bottles with just one (or less than one) measure in. It is time to banish those things from your house and claim some space in your cupboards.

Find all your alcohol, pull it from every nook and cranny around the house, and lose what you don't use. You can either have a fun cocktail night to use it up or you can give your drains a good clean. Whatever you do, make sure you drink responsibly and recycle the bottles.

MEDICINE

Medicine finds its way into various areas of a home, the bathroom, bedroom, the junk drawer, in your bag. It is important to have access to medication when you are out and about but in the home it is much easier to manage if it is in one place. The kitchen is a good place as it is centrally located and has more space for you to be able to store it safely.

- To start this activity, you need to collect all your medicine together.
- Check the expiry date, get rid of anything out of date or if you know you no longer need it (old prescription meds etc).
- Then group and organise your medicines by type – painkillers, children's, plasters etc.

Once you have sorted it look for a box or boxes you can use to contain it and then a place to store it. High up cupboards are useful for storing medication, you don't need to access it regularly and it keeps it out of reach of little hands.

JUNK DRAWER

Everyone has one, sometimes called the junk drawer or even the 'third drawer down' (it seems to be true in a lot of houses). It may seem overwhelming to do but the things in this drawer will easily fall into categories.

Give yourself some room and empty the contents, do a quick sort - useful and useless; keep the first and lose the second.
Then group all the same items together, which will include some of the following:

- batteries
- keys
- money
- takeaway menus
- pens / pencils
- light bulbs
- and the odd screwdriver
- ...the list goes on.

Once you have grouped them you can see what you need to store. Some of these things might have a home somewhere else in which case put them there. The thing to remember with a junk drawer is it is full of useful things you may need to have to hand, so even though you have a toolbox in the shed, it is handy to have a couple of screwdrivers in the house for changing the battery on a toy etc. Give them a place to belong.

This drawer is never going to be beautiful, but it can be practical and organised. Containing items in small containers is the key to achieving this. You don't need to buy any boxes to partition your drawer, use what you have; shoe boxes, the tupperware box with no lid, old mobile phone boxes etc.

CHAPTER 5

BATHROOM

Storage tends to be limited in a bathroom, so items collect on surfaces and give the room a cluttered feeling. These activities will transform it into a calmer space for you to enjoy. This chapter will look at:

Toiletries

Make Up

Towels

TOILETRIES

Toiletries easily accumulate, lovely to buy, to give and receive as gifts, it is not surprising you end up with more than you need. This is a quick activity to start clearing some clutter from your bathroom.

- Collect all your toiletries in one place, start by categorising them (shampoo, deodorant, soap etc), it helps you see what you have. Now check through each category one by one.
- Discard any products you bought, tried but didn't like. They are a sunk cost; the money has already been spent and if you didn't like them when you first used them that will not change.
- If you have a collection of miniatures from hotels, either make a note to use them at home or when you travel (make a travel box to contain them), or let them go, they are just taking up space.

- If you have any empty perfume bottles that are nice to look at, but just collect dust they can go straight into the recycling.

Once you have been through all your toiletries pull out the ones you want to use first, these are the ones you need to have easy access to. Locate these in your shower or by your bath. The rest of your toiletries should be treated as back stock, so either find space in your bathroom cupboards or if there is no room find a space near your bathroom where you could locate them; making your bathroom environment less cluttered (and maybe making space for a few candles).

MAKE UP

Did you know make up 'goes off'? The little picture of a pot with a number and then M is how many months you are meant to keep it once you have opened it. If you are not sure when you bought it there are a couple of websites, you can use to help you.

checkfresh.com
checkcosmetic.net

Entering the brand and product code gives you the date it was produced, this gives you a good place to start.

Get all your make up together and start by sorting it all into categories, it helps you to see what you have. Look at each category in turn.

- Anything old (you can check with the above sites or you may know), that has dried up or run out can go, you will probably find this includes a lot of things you no longer use.

- Any additional items you know you don't use anymore as the colour is wrong or you don't like can be put into your goodbye pile too.

Well done, you have transformed your make up collection.

Ready for more?

Once you know what you have you can look at how you store your make up. Make up bags are not the best storage for make up (unless you are travelling), it all gets muddled up, makes it difficult to find what you want and inevitably a powder breaks and covers everything.

There are lots of great make up storage systems you can invest in or you can simply use small boxes in a drawer to keep items in their categories and contained. If you are going to invest the best systems are acrylic ones as they allow you to see what you have and display it beautifully.

TOWELS

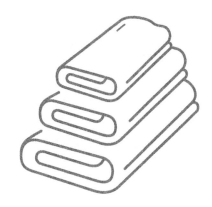

You may be lucky enough to have storage space for your towels in your bathroom, or you might have an airing cupboard. Wherever you keep them you will probably have too many and find it difficult to get to the ones you want.

Towels are difficult to throw away even when they lose that lovely fluffiness, it seems such a waste, but getting rid of the ones you no longer need will make sure you have room to store the ones you do.

- Pull out your favourites, matching sets, or those you use regularly.
- Look at the number of people in your house and how many towels you have, two each is a good base to start (excluding swimming / beach towels). Make sure you have a guest set as well.

- Now to store your towels. You can roll or fold, there is no superior way it just depends which you prefer and works in the space you have.
- Arrange your towels in sets (if you have matching ones) or by type (hand, bath etc).
- Label your cupboard, it will help you keep them organised and make it easy to find the right ones.

Any old towels can be donated (see donate chapter) or you can cut them up to use as cleaning cloths.

CHAPTER 6

BEDROOM

A place of tranquillity, or that is how it should be. There are numerous studies which show a cluttered bedroom can not only impact your ability to go to sleep but also your sleep pattern. The problem with bedrooms is there are a lot of things that create clutter; clothes pile up easily and it is out of sight in the day, so easy to forget. There are plenty of items you can separate out to tackle individually, this chapter will cover:

Bedside Table   Clothes

Jewellery   Bedding

Socks

Underwear

Swimwear

BEDSIDE TABLE

Your bed and the surrounding area should be as clutter free as possible, unfortunately the bedside table attracts various essential and non-essential items. Think about what you really need there, it isn't a collection of books or tickets from a show or some old glasses you no longer use; time to transform.

Take everything out the drawers and off the surface. Pick up everything you want by the side of your bed, things could include:

- the book you are currently reading,
- a space for a glass of water,
- somewhere to keep your glasses,
- a place for any jewellery you take off at night,
- a box of tissues.

If you have the luxury of drawers there maybe a few other bits you can store like tablets or hand cream but try to keep the top as clear as possible.

Lots of studies have shown having a phone or device by your bed interrupts your sleep, so if you can bear to be parted from it, plug that in somewhere else. Everything else needs to go, find good homes for it all.

JEWELLERY

Jewellery can be a difficult item to declutter and organise, even if it doesn't have a large monetary value it can have a huge sentimental one. Deal with these two categories as separate activities, non-sentimental items can be organised in 10 minutes, but the rest will take longer.

Non sentimental items
Pick up each piece and see how you feel about it, would you wear it right now? If not, why not? Any odd earrings missing the pair? Sort it all into three piles:

- Keep, these are the items you wear all the time.
- Donate, anything you know you don't or won't wear; you can give them to a friend or family member and if you have some valuable items you could sell them (remember to be realistic about doing this).

- Review, this is for all those bits you are not sure about. Find a place to put these items and give yourself a deadline to wear them (a month or two). If you have worn and enjoyed them by then move them to your collection, if not donate them for someone else to enjoy.

If you come across any sentimental pieces don't get stuck on what to do with it, put it to one side to assess when you address your sentimental jewellery.

Sentimental items

These are harder items to make decisions on, you may need more than 10 minutes. Give yourself time to sit with your sentimental jewellery. It can be hard to let it go, so you will have to think about dealing with these items in a different way.

- The first question to answer (honestly) is will you wear it? If the answer is yes then it can go into your collection. If the answer is no, these questions might help you decide what to do with it.
- Are you able to gift it to a member of your family who will enjoy wearing it?
- Can you have it repurposed / made into something else you would wear?
- Is it something you want to give to your children as part of their inheritance?

It is important to remember the person who gave / left you the item did so for you to enjoy, not to hold onto through a sense of obligation; make a choice that makes you feel happy.

Ready for more?

You might have a good storage system for your jewellery, but if not and it is all tangled up in the drawer here are a couple of options that work well.

'Command decoration clips' (meant for fairy lights) are great for hanging necklaces, stick them to the back of your wardrobe door.

Jewellery boxes are a great way to store your jewellery, but you need to make sure they are fit for purpose i.e., if you have lots of earrings and necklaces making sure you have the right compartments for those items. Stackers boxes are very compact, and you can buy each layer separately allowing you to get exactly what you need.

SOCKS

This an easy place to start your transformation journey; they are simple to sort and get into order.

- Get all your socks together (you can challenge the whole family to join in and sort their own).
- Pull them onto your hand and check for holes, if they have any they can be thrown away.
- Discard any that you know you don't wear because they are uncomfortable (everyone has at least one pair), or any that you don't wear because you don't like the colour (maybe the white isn't as white as you want).

Now it is time to pair them up (unless you like to wear odd socks), any that don't have a matching pair can go.

Now look at how many you have and how many you need, remember there are only 7 days in the week. You can make room in your drawer by letting some of them go.

Pick out your favourites to start and aim for no more than 10 pairs of everyday socks.

The best way to store your socks is to roll them (so you are not stretching the elastic), Sock organisers are great to stop them becoming a jumble in your drawer, with the added advantage of helping to limit how many you keep.

UNDERWEAR

This is an essential item and usually the last thing anyone thinks about getting organised, but it can bring so much joy when you take the time to do it. It can change the way you feel in the morning when you get dressed, a good way to spark joy before you even leave your bedroom.

- Pull all your underwear out of the drawer and start to sort through.
- Grab the bras you don't wear (the ones that are uncomfortable), put them in a pile of things to go. If they are in good condition you can donate them (see donate chapter).
- Look at your pants, discard any with holes, that don't fit, where the elastic has gone or any that are discoloured.

Now you will have the underwear you want to wear. An underwear organiser will keep it contained and organised.

SWIMWEAR

This is a very seasonal item (unless you are an avid swimmer or have young children). The first thing to do is to grab them all together, then check through them all.

- Any that are past their best - frayed, elastic gone or have gone a bit see through (hold the bottoms up to the light and check) need to go.
- Any you keep as your back up but know you never reach for because you don't really like them should go.
- And of course, any that don't fit.

It is great to keep them all together and stored in one place, a box will help you contain them, and you can pop it in a drawer or on a shelf.

CLOTHES

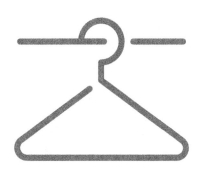

Clothes are impossible to do in their entirety in 10 minutes, here is a quick activity you can do to kick off the process.

Pull out the clothes you don't wear; the ones you have not worn (and you know why). The hard bit of this is to be honest with yourself and accept they are no longer for you. Reasons you never reach for them can include:

- your arms / tummy etc look funny,
- it's itchy,
- it's too tight round the neck,
- you don't like the colour,

reasons you held onto them can include:
- it was expensive,
- it still has the tag,
- it is designer,
- you will fit back into it,
- it feels wasteful.

Don't stop to think about it, don't question how much you paid, just be honest. Your wardrobe should make you feel happy when you open it rather than burdened. So donate, let someone else find and treasure them. .

Ready for more?
If you want to completely transform your wardrobe here are steps you can take.

Halve your wardrobe by separating into seasonal items, this helps with the process of sorting and separating things.

Make even more room by investing in some velvet hangers. They are slim giving you lots of space to store your clothes and they don't slide off and end up at the bottom of your wardrobe.

Take each item of clothing out one by one and hold it up. If you feel happy and are smiling when you hold it, it should go on the keep pile. If you are not (and you feel your shoulders slumping) it is probably time to let it go. If you are still struggling, go through previous list above with each item and be honest (having a good, honest friend close to hand helps).

Put your clothes into your wardrobe organised by type - skirts, trousers, dresses etc. If you want it to look even more beautiful organise each section by colour.

BEDDING

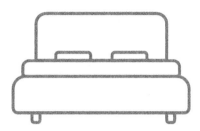

You may be lucky enough to have an airing or laundry cupboard, but if not storing bedding in the room you use it is a good way to organise. Before you think about storage, look at what you have.

A good rule of thumb for bedding is one for the bed and one for the wash; you will probably have more than two sets per bed, so to start...

- Categorise your bedding, sheets together sorted into size, duvet covers together sorted into size along with any matching pillowcases.
- Pick out your favourites, the ones you always reach for (remember you will have a set on every bed).
- Pick out the ones you never use, or that are threadbare or discoloured; donate the good quality ones and use the rest as rags.
- For duvet covers that don't have matching pillows, find pillowcases you like to use with it and make a set.

Once you have the ones you want, you can look at where to store them.

- Keep duvets and pillowcases together; either pop everything in one pillowcase or fold the pillowcases inside the duvet.
- If you have a linen cupboard, store by bedding type and size, labelling each shelf.
- If you don't have a cupboard store them in the relevant bedroom, a drawer, shelf or even under the bed in a zip up bag.
- Remember to keep a guest set or two.

Having a 'one in one out' rule helps to maintain this area; when you buy new bedding make sure you know which set is going to leave.

CHAPTER 7

HOME OFFICE

You may not have a home office; in which case these items will probably be in your kitchen or spare room. This chapter includes the following:

Pens

Manuals

Wrapping Paper

PENS

It is frustrating grabbing a pen to find it doesn't work, this is a fun activity you can do alone or with your family (set a timer to see how quickly you can do it).

- Run around the house and collect all the pens, felt tips and pencils into one place.
- Take a large sheet of paper and just scribble, if there isn't a nice strong mark get rid of it.
- If pencils are small and broken throw them.
- If the lead falls out after you sharpen, it is likely the lead is broken all the way through, you can let those go.

When you have finished you should have a pile of writing and drawing things that work and you can place around the house where you need them.

MANUALS

Do you keep them? They have important information in surely. What if....? This is an area where you can be ruthless.

All the information you need about anything you have ever bought is available online. You can find it on the manufacturers website or there are countless videos on YouTube if you ever need to find out 'how to...?'

You can throw them away with confidence. They will be taking up valuable space in a drawer or cupboard in your office / kitchen and you really don't need them.

Still need convincing? Think about the last time you looked at any of them.

WRAPPING PAPER

Having a stock of cards and wrapping paper is a great way to make sure you are organised and prepared for anything. Having them all in one place makes life a lot easier but wrapping paper rolls are tricky to store.

For this activity, research and buy a storage box or bag that is specifically designed for wrapping paper rolls. It is worth investing in one, it prevents you having rolls of paper in a plastic bag shoved at the back of a cupboard (that fall over every time you open it). You can store the box under the sofa, bed or in your office, accessible but not in prime location.

The same with cards, get a box to store all your cards in one place; if you want to go one step further you can organise them by occasion.

CHAPTER 8

CHILDREN'S ROOMS

Children's things are usually spread around the house, in their bedroom, playroom or even kitchen. This chapter will deal with the main culprits of clutter in your children's rooms, it will cover:

Toys

Artwork

Books

TOYS

It is difficult to keep toys sorted and organised, getting your children involved can help or hinder the process depending on how old they are and how ready they are to let things go, so pick your time.

If you want to get your children involved doing it prior to Christmas or a birthday helps; talk to your children about making space for new toys and what giving their old ones to another child to love would mean.

Alternatively, do it without your children, spiriting away any toys you know they no longer play with. Whichever way you do it make sure you get them out the house quickly, any toys sat by the door is a sure way for them to become their new favourite toy.

Trying to sort and organise all the toys will take far longer than 10 minutes, this activity is one to kick off the process. It doesn't need to be a big organised clear and sort - just go with your gut.

- Pick out all the toys with missing pieces and broken bits, put them in the bin (recycling what you can).
- Pick out anything that is not being played with, but in good condition and donate (see donate chapter).

Well done, you have kicked off the process and hopefully cleared a little bit of plastic from your lives.

Ready for more?

Contain and label are two words you need most when it comes to toys. Having storage available that will allow you to contain and organise their toys is important, but before you rush out and buy anything have a look at what toys you have and what storage you have available.

- Categorising toys is the first step, making sure you have similar types of toys together i.e., all the cars or vehicles, all the musical instruments, puzzles etc.
- Next look at containing what you have, find boxes and containers which will work.
- The last stage is to label them clearly, this helps you remember where things go but also helps your children keep things tidy. Making labels from pictures of their actual toys can act as a useful visual reminder.

ARTWORK

Whether you find it easy to spirit things away to the recycle bin or not you are probably holding onto far too much of your child's artwork. It is difficult to let go as it feels like it captures a moment in time, which you don't want to forget.

Fast forward a few years; you will either have boxes of it around your house or in your loft and your child will have left home. Fast forward again to the point you decide to give it to them; will they be happy to see all of it or will it become a burden for them to keep?

You could be ruthless and just throw it all away, but I am sure they would like to see some of it when they are older, but maybe a few select pieces not boxes of it. This activity is to kick start a process to keep it manageable and organised; once you have got it working well you will feel confident about tackling any historical art.

- Keep a small folder for each child and put their work in it.
- When it is full, go through it with your child and choose a couple of favourites.
- At the end of the year reduce it to a select few and put them into their memory box (see sentimental items chapter).
- Remember to write the date of anything you keep when you get it - even if it is just the year.

You can happily recycle the rest, even if you have to do it in the dead of night. Think about not creating future clutter for your children; if you can I am sure they will thank you for it.

BOOKS

Children's bookshelves often get to the point of overflowing with books stacked up. There are usually a mix of books, some that have been read but they don't like, some they love, as well as ones that they may have loved but are now below their reading ability. This quick 10 minute activity can be done with your children, or alone.

Depending on how many shelves you have you might want to do one a day, so it is not overwhelming.

- Empty the shelf and have a quick look at each book, you and your child will know immediately if it should go on the keep or donate pile.
- Once you have the sorted take the donate ones to the local school and pop the rest back on the shelf.

Ready for more?

If you want to help your children rediscover books, it is good to reorganise the whole bookcase. You can organise books by author, category or even colour, separating non-fiction (then into categories) and fiction (sorted by author) is a good way to help your child find the books they want.

Alternatively, you can try book rotation, changing books over every few weeks; it reduces the books on the shelf making them easier to see and makes it feel like they have new books.

CHAPTER 9

SENTIMENTAL

No one can tell you what is sentimental as it is such a personal thing, but without a place to put items they end up lost in a drawer. These items stop you in your tracks when you start trying to get organised, partly because you start to reminisce but mostly because you don't know what to do with them. Having a place to put items you want to keep is the key to prevent this from happening.

This 10 minute activity is to research and buy yourself a memory box; spend as much or as little as you want, just make sure it is beautiful and there is somewhere accessible to put it..

When buying a box make sure it is big enough, but not so big you cannot find anywhere to store it and you end up keeping everything. Look for boxes that are 20-30cm for each dimension. It is important to work out where you will keep it so you can make sure it will fit.

It should be somewhere accessible, somewhere easy to reach making it is easy to put things in and easy to access when you want to look at it.

Get one for every member of the family. It is a great place to keep your children's artwork and a handful of school books and helps to manage how much you keep.

CHAPTER 10

OUT & ABOUT

Getting organised doesn't always have to be in your home, there are a few things you can do when you are out and about, waiting for the swimming lesson to finish or on the train to work. This chapter covers:

Purse

Pockets

Phone

PURSE

This is a quick activity you can do whilst you are out and about or at home.

- Empty it out.
- Throw away receipts you no longer need - or if you want to hold onto them put them to one side to file.
- Check your membership cards are all in date - get rid of any that are not.
- Throw away any loyalty cards that are over 6 months and just have one stamp, if you don't go there regularly you don't need it.

Now pop back in all the things you really do need, hopefully it will be much easier to close.

POCKETS

Pockets collect so much stuff in them, when do you ever stop to empty them out? This is a really quick activity you can do whilst you are out.

- Empty your pockets.
- Throw away any rubbish, old receipts tissues, scraps of paper.
- If you have lots of pockets, put things you always want to have available (masks, lip balms, trolley token) in your less used pockets, so they don't get caught up with daily items.
- Put everything else back in your main pockets.

Find a bin and make sure you throw the rubbish away.

PHONE

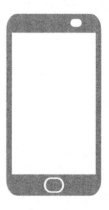

There is so much you could organise with your phone, but to keep it simple this activity focuses on making sure you have the information you need at your fingertips. Despite this piece of technology becoming a vital part of our lives, we often don't take time to get it organised. The best bit about this activity is you can do it without leaving your seat.

- Go through your phone and delete the apps you no longer use.
- Move the ones you use most frequently to the home screen.
- Make folders for your apps organising them into categories; here are some ideas: travel / shopping /social / finance / utilities / entertainment / games / lifestyle / productivity / education

If you fancy something different organise your apps by colour, giving you a rainbow screen (you may be sceptical at this approach, but it really works, companies spend vast amounts of money to plug into that bit of your brain that recognises brands).

Whatever you do it will take a bit of time to get used to, but you will find it will save you time having the things you need just one click away.

CHAPTER 11

DONATE

'One man's trash is another man's treasure.'

This chapter gives you some ideas of places to whom you can donate your unwanted items. This is not a comprehensive list of every organisation available and is correct at the time of writing.

CDs and DVDs
Take them to your local charity shop or try to sell them on any of these sites - We Buy Books, Music Magpie or Zapper - or recycle them at your local recycling centre.

General
Take items to your local charity shop, if you have too many or can't get there, I Collect Clothes will pick up clothes, books, toys, electrical items (see their website for the full list). Book a slot on their website and they will come and collect from your door.

Furniture

The British Heart foundation will pick up large pieces of furniture from your home if they have a fire safety certificate. Head to their website, fill out your details and they will contact you with a date to come and collect.

Glasses

A lot of opticians no longer accept old glasses (Vision Aid Overseas have stopped their recycling scheme) but these organisations still are.

Peep Eyewear- will upcycle, restore, and resell them and give a donation to Lions Club, or you can send them directly to Lions Clubs who send them to various places including - Medico France and to eye clinics in Papua New Guinea, Sri Lanka, Ghana, Nigeria, and Nepal.

Children's Shoes

Children's shoes can be sent to Sal's Shoes, they package them up and send them to children who don't have any.

Children's Toys

Young Planet App is a fantastic app you can use to list and find children's toys for free. It is simple to list an item, you just take a photo, add a title and description and you are all done.

Underwear

Smalls for All are a charity that collect and distribute underwear to women and children in Africa. If you have any 'gently worn' bras pop them in an envelope and send them to the address on their website.

Wellies

Hunter Boots will take your old wellies, process, and shred them and make them into playground surfacing, roads, and lots of other things. They have teamed up with First Mile who will pick up your old boots for free. The process is simple, go to Hunter Boots website, fill out a form, choose to pick up or drop off, then pop them in a box and label it up. Not only do your boots get reused but Hunter boots also send you a code for 15% off some new ones.

Women's Clothes

Give Your Best are a charity who work with women refugees to provide them a place to choose clothes they would like to wear. They have a simple process on their website, you take photos of your item and then when it has been 'shopped' you post it directly to the person who chose it.

Dress for Success are a great charity if you have any new or barely worn work clothes, they make sure they go to women who are trying to find work. Contact them and arrange for clothes to be sent by post, courier, or taxi.

INDEX

Printed in Great Britain
by Amazon

78472680R00058